Quiet Moments for Mothers

Compiled by

JOYCE & NORMAN WRIGHT

HARVEST HOUSE PUBLISHERS
EUGENE, OREGON 97402

Quiet Moments for Mothers

A Tribute to My Mother

I would like to tell you about a very special mother—
my own mother, Amelia Nette Theresa Cornelius Wright.
Born in 1900, Mom grew up in the horse-and-buggy days
and lived to hear about the space probe to Mars, as well as
men walking on the moon. Her childhood spent on a South
Dakota farm formed her positive character as she plowed
corn in the family's fields, skated to school on the frozen
Sioux River during harsh winters, and held a light for her
father as he built one of America's first homemade tractors.

Mom married her first husband, a World War I airplane
mechanic, when she was 19. After the marriage, the young
couple began an odyssey of moves that would eventually
take them westward to California. They drove a rickety
old car that also doubled as their sleeping quarters, and
cooked their food in a pan on two stones over a fire. They
eventually settled like pioneers in the hills above
Hollywood and began to build their first home, which
had a down payment of ten dollars for the lot. Mom's
farming background came in handy as she planted fruit
trees, vegetables, and her favorite flowers.

Four years after Mom's first son, Paul, was born in 1930, tragedy struck when her husband suddenly died of a stroke. In 1937, Mom married my dad, a widower, and I was born when Mom was 37 years old and Dad was 49. Mom worked hard raising Paul and me as well as keeping up our three rental homes. She encouraged us to enjoy life and championed the values of honesty, hard work, and a thorough education. Both of my parents made sacrifices to give us the experiences and opportunities that had not been available to them as children. We went on trips and were given music lessons. As a family, we saw practically every movie produced in Hollywood during the '40s. If Dad was busy working, Mom filled in playing baseball and taking me hunting and fishing.

Mom was a woman whose values reflected her early years as well as her family's background. Wanting us to develop our potential to the fullest, she encouraged us, helped us in any way possible when we struggled, corrected us when necessary, and demonstrated compassion. She spoke her mind and was definite, but she listened and considered others' opinions and beliefs. Mom passed on a strong legacy, a rich heritage from her side of the family. As a result, my brother and I have a better sense of who we are individually and as a family.

Mom was widowed a second time in 1960 when my dad was killed in an auto accident at the age of 72, yet she still continued to embrace life. She took art lessons and painted scenic and still-life pictures, amazing even herself with the latent talent. She traveled to England, France, Germany, and Switzerland. Not just another sightseer, Mom smuggled Bibles into Moscow, rode in a kayak, danced with an Alaskan sourdough in Nome, and went to the top of the Eiffel Tower in Paris. Even into her nineties, she continued to raise the flowers she had always loved and wrote her own life history.

Although Mom was growing older, two things never wore out: her spirit and her love of family—her children, grandchildren, great-grandchildren, and nephews and nieces of at least three generations. In October of 1993, Mom received her final assignment. Her work here was complete after 93 years. In the home-going service for Mom, whom I miss, I recall the statement, "When you say good-bye to a loved one who is a believer, remember at that moment they are saying hello to Jesus Christ." My mom is there in heaven along with my son, Matthew.

I am so thankful for my mother who influenced and loved me.

H. Norman Wright

Quiet Moments for Mothers

Motherhood over the centuries has been celebrated by many famous writers. Hopefully their words will let you know that you are not forgotten nor taken for granted, but rather appreciated, valued, and desperately needed.

The honoring of mothers involves the recognition of their influence on the lives of their children. The following quotes and poems illustrate the wide spectrum of the way in which mothers touch and transform lives. There are also a few words of encouragement to help you keep pushing on in your calling as a mother.

Faith of our mothers, Christian faith,

In truth beyond our stumbling creeds,

Still serve the home and save the church,

And breathe thy spirit through our deeds;

Faith of our mothers, Christian faith,

We will be true to thee til death.

MARTIN LUTHER

When God thought of Mother, he must have laughed

with satisfaction, and framed it quickly—

so rich, so deep, so divine, so full of soul, power,

and beauty, was the conception.

HENRY WARD BEECHER

*N*othing can compare in beauty,

and wonder, and admirableness,

and divinity itself, to the

silent work in obscure dwellings

of faithful women bringing

their children to honor and

virtue and piety.

HENRY WARD BEECHER

A mother is not a person

to lean on but a person to make

leaning unnecessary.

DOROTHY FISCHER

There was a place in childhood,

that I remember well,

And there a voice of sweetest tone,

bright fairy tales did tell.

And gentle words, and fond embrace,

were given with joy to me,

When I was in that happy place

upon my mother's knee.

SAMUEL LOVER

The memory of my mother

will always be a blessing to me.

THOMAS EDISON

$\mathcal{D}$o not forsake your mother's teaching.

Bind them upon your heart forever;

fasten them around your neck. When you walk,

they will guide you; when you sleep, they will watch

over you; when you awake, they will speak to you.

PROVERBS 6:20-22

Mighty is the force of motherhood,

it transforms all things by its vital heat;

it turns timidity into fierce courage,

and dreadless defiance into tremulous submission.

It turns thoughtlessness into foresight,

and yet stills all anxiety into calm content.

It makes selfishness become self-denial, and gives even

to hard vanity the glance of admiring love.

Hundreds of dewdrops to greet the dawn;

Hundreds of lambs in the purple clover,

Hundreds of butterflies on the lawn;

But only one mother the wide world over.

GEORGE COOPER

All mothers are rich

when they love their own.

There are no poor mothers,

no ugly ones, no old ones.

Their love is always the most beautiful

of the joys. And when they seem

most sad it needs but a kiss which

they receive or give to turn all

their tears into stars in the

depth of their eyes.

MAURICE MAETERLINCK

They say

that man is mighty;

He governs land and sea,

He wields a mighty scepter

O'er lesser powers that be.

But a mightier power and stronger

Man from his throne has hurled,

For the hand that rocks the cradle

Is the hand that rules

the world.

WILLIAM ROSS WALLACE

$\mathcal{D}$id you ever receive a letter which warmed your heart by the memories it brought to mind, and which dimmed your eyes with tears? Such a letter Timothy received one time from Paul. In the letter Paul said, "I call to remembrance the unfeigned faith that is in thee, which dwelt first in thy grandmother Lois, and thy mother Eunice; and I am persuaded that in thee also." As Timothy read these words I am quite sure that his heart was warm with tender childhood memories, and his eyes misty. Then he re-read on through the long beautiful letter, which hinged its message upon these

words. Because of the faith of

his mother before him, because

of the faith she had implanted

within Timothy, Paul was

pleading with him to "stir up

the gift of God which is in thee."

A godly heritage: that was

Timothy's precious

gift from his mother.

LAURA MERRIHEW ADAMS

I wear for you, Mother, sweet violets of blue,

That waft me to girlhood and visions of you.

They hold in their perfume, mysterious power

To bring you close to me, our symbol this flower.

I wear for you, Mother, sweet violets of blue;

They draw me in memory to your guidance true.

I liken their fragrance to your tenderness,

Your soul strength pervasive, and your nobleness.

SERENA TRUMAN ROBINSON

Lord who ordains for mankind

Benignant toils and tender cares,

We thank thee for the ties that bind

The mother to the child she bears...

And grateful for the blessing given

With that dear infant on her knee,

She trains the eye to look to heaven,

The voice to lisp a prayer to Thee...

All-Gracious! grant to those who bear

A mother's charge, the strength and light

To guide the feet that own their care

In ways of Love and Truth and Right.

WILLIAM CULLEN BRYANT

A picture memory brings to me:

I look across the years and see

Myself beside my mother's knee.

I feel her gentle hand restrain

My selfish moods and know again

A child's wrong sense

of wrong and pain.

But wiser now, a man gray grown,

My childhood's needs

are better known,

My mother's chastening love I own.

JOHN GREENLEAF WHITTIER

$\mathcal{A}$ Bible open by her bed, why? What was it?

What did it mean? Only a book? Her source of love

and kindness, patience and strength, her love of God

and His holy Son, her joy, her wonder at God's world.

She passed it all on to me. How she loved me!

AUTHOR UNKNOWN

From my mother, I learned the value of prayer, how
to have dreams and believe I would make them come true.
While my father was filled with dreams of making
something of himself, she had a drive to help my brother
and me make something of ourselves.

RONALD REAGAN

For the mother is and must be, whether she knows it
or not, the greatest, strongest, and most lasting teacher
her children have. Other influences come and go,
but hers is continual; and by the opinion men have
of women we can generally judge
of the sort of mother they had.

HANNAH WHITALL SMITH

$\mathcal{A}$ mother...fills a place

so great that there isn't an

angel in heaven who wouldn't

be glad to give a bushel of

diamonds to come down here

and take her place.

BILLY SUNDAY

Because I feel, that in the Heavens above,

The angels, whispering to one another,

Can find, among their burning terms of love,

None so devotional as that of "Mother,"

Therefore by that dear name I long have called you.

EDGAR ALLEN POE

For when you looked into my mother's eyes

you knew, as if He had told you,

why God sent her into the world—

it was to open the minds of all who looked,

to beautiful thoughts.

JAMES M. BARRIE

We never know the love of the parent

till we become parents ourselves. When we

first bend over the cradle of our own child,

God throws back the temple door, and reveals

to us the sacredness and mystery of a

father's and a mother's love to ourselves.

HENRY WARD BEECHER

The mother love is like God's love;

He loves us not because we are lovable,

but because it is His nature to love,

and because we are His children.

EARL RINEY

Prayer is over —

to my pillow

With a good-night kiss I creep,

Scarcely waking while I whisper,

"Now I lay me down to sleep."

Then my mother, o'er me bending,

Prays in earnest words, but mild,

"Hear my prayers, O heavenly Father,

Bless, oh, bless

my precious child."

ANONYMOUS

The woman

who creates and sustains

a home, and under whose

hands children grow up

to be strong, pure men and women,

is a creator second only to God.

HELEN JACKSON

Yours were the hands that held me first of all,

Yours were the lips that taught mine own to smile,

Yours were the eyes that watched my every step,

And yours the heart that showed me Love worth while;

Whatever good men see, in part or whole,

Is but the dear reflection of your soul!

When others laughed at all my dreams, You held those dreams—

and me—close to your loving breast,

Giving me strength to try, and when I failed,

Your faith alone stood firm above the rest.

For you believed some day I would succeed—

The finest spur that any man could need!

And so, to-day, though far from what I've sought,

The goal unreached, the prize as yet unwon,

Your hands still hold on high Belief and Trust,

As once they held my baby self—your son.

The Mother-Faith knows naught of doubt or fear,

But goes serenely on, year after year!

EVERARD JACK APPLETON

Rocking My Child

The sea its millions of waves

is rocking, divine,

hearing the loving seas,

I'm rocking my child.

The wandering wind in the night

is rocking the fields of wheat,

hearing the loving winds,

I'm rocking my child.

God the father his thousands of worlds

is rocking without a sound.

Feeling his hand in the shadows,

I'm rocking my child.

GABRIELA MISTAL

To My Mother

You too, my mother, read my rhymes

For love of unforgotten times,

And you may chance to hear once more

The little feet along the floor.

How many cares does

a mother's heart know?

Nobody knows but Mother.

How many joys from

her mother love flow?

Nobody knows but Mother.

How many prayers for each little white bed?

How many tears for her babes

has she shed?

How many kisses for each curly head?

Nobody knows but Mother.

Robert Louis Stevenson

My
Mother's
Garden

Her heart is like her garden,
Old-fashioned, quaint and sweet,
With here a wealth of blossoms,
And there a still retreat.
Sweet violets are hiding,
We know as we pass by,
And lilies, pure as angel thoughts,
Are opening somewhere nigh.

Forget-me-nots there linger,
to full perfection brought,
And there bloom purple pansies
In many a tender thought.
There love's own roses blossom,
As from enchanted ground,
And lavish perfume exquisite
The whole glad year around.
And in that quiet garden—
The garden of her heart—
Songbirds are always singing
Their songs of cheer apart.
And from it floats forever,
O'ercoming sin and strife,
Sweet as the breath of roses blown,
The fragrance of her life.

ALICE E. ALLEN

call her blessed

$\mathscr{A}$ wife of noble character who can find?...

In her hand she holds the distaff and grasps the spindle
with her fingers. She opens her arms to the poor and
extends her hands to the needy.

Her children arise and call her blessed....

PROVERBS 31:10, 19, 20, 28

$\mathscr{A}$ woman giving birth to a child has pain
because her time has come; but when her baby
is born she forgets the anguish because of her joy
that a child is born into the world.

JOHN 16:21

The Wonderful Mother

God made a wonderful mother,

A mother who never grows old;

He made her smile of the sunshine,

And He molded her heart of pure gold;

In her eyes He placed bright shining stars,

On her cheeks, fair roses you see;

God made a wonderful mother,

And He gave that dear mother to me.

PAT O'REILLY

My mother was the source from which I derived the guiding principles of my life.

JOHN WESLEY

A Tribute to Christian Mothers

Only God Himself fully appreciates

the influence of a Christian mother in the

molding of the character in her children...

If we had more Christian mothers we would

have less delinquency, less immorality,

less ungodliness and fewer broken homes.

The influence of a mother in her home upon

the lives of her children cannot be measured.

They know and absorb her example and

attitudes when it comes to questions of

honesty, temperance, kindness and industry...

BILLY GRAHAM

My Altar

The things in life that are worthy

Were born in my mother's breast

And breathed into mine by the magic

Of the love her life expressed.

The years that have brought me to manhood

Have taken her far from me;

But memory keeps me from straying

Too far from my mother's knee.

JOHN H. STYLES, JR.

The most glorious sight that one ever sees beneath the stars is the sight of worthy motherhood.

GEORGE W TRUETT

A true mother is not merely a provider, housekeeper, comforter, or companion. A true mother is primarily and essentially a trainer.

RUTH BELL GRAHAM

No nation ever had a better friend than the mother who taught her children to pray.

ANONYMOUS

A mother

is a chalice, the vessel

without which no human being

has ever been born. *S*he is created

to be a life-bearer, cooperating with her

husband and with *G*od in the making of a child.

*W*hat a solemn responsibility. *W*hat an

unspeakable privilege—a vessel

divinely prepared for the

*M*aster's use.

ELISABETH ELLIOT

Mothers, You Are Great!

I know of no more permanent imprint on a life than the one made by mothers. I guess that's why Mother's Day always leaves me a little nostalgic. Not simply because my mother has gone on (and heaven's probably cleaner because of it!), but because that's the one day the real heroines of our world get the credit they deserve. Hats off to every one of you!

More than any statesman or teacher, more than any minister or physician, more than any film star, athlete, business person, author, scientist, civic leader, entertainer, or military hero… you are the most influential person in your child's life.

Never doubt that fact!

Not even when the dishes in the sink resemble the Leaning Tower… or the washing machine gets choked and dies… or the place looks a wreck and nobody at home stops to say, "Thanks, Mom. You're great."

It's still worth it. You are great. This is your time to make the most significant contribution in all of life. Don't sell it short. In only a few years it will all be a memory. Make it a good one.

CHARLES SWINDOLL

My Mom, Too!

You raised them well, loving and kind, and to great amazement God made one mine. He knew He could create and mold godly men through you, and in knowing you'd do a fine job, He gave you two!

But the Lord took you even further, though you're unaware, and gave you extra love for me that you're always glad to share. You're a true example of how He wants us to stand—firm and tall, and that is why I call you my *mom*, not my mother-in-law.

Thank you Mom for being who God intended you to be, and thank you Lord for giving her especially to me.

KELLY S.

I remember my mother's prayers, and they have always followed me. They have clung to me all of my life.

ABRAHAM LINCOLN

*T*hese commandments that I give you today are to be upon your hearts. Impress them on your children. Talk about them when you sit at home and when you walk along the road, when you lie down and when you get up.

DEUTERONOMY 6:6, 7

*T*here is no higher height to which humanity can attain than that occupied by a converted, heaven-inspired, praying mother.

ANONYMOUS

A woman who fears and reverences God

shall be greatly praised. Praise her for the

many fine things she does. These good deeds

of hers shall bring her honor and

recognition from people of importance.

PROVERBS 31:30, 31 TLB

*Y*outh fades, love droops,

the leaves of friendship fall;

A mother's secret hope

outlives them all.

OLIVER WENDELL HOLMES

To Mother

You painted no Madonnas

On chapel walls in Rome,

But with a touch diviner

You lived one in your home...

You built no great cathedrals

That centuries applaud

But with a grace exquisite

Your life cathedraled God...

T. W. FESSENDEN

A mother's days are made wearisome by the wants

and frequent waywardness of little children, and her

nights are often made wakeful by their illnesses.

But while those little ones are burdens, they are

such lovable bundles of graceful curves and such

constant sources of surprise and joy.

RALPH SOCKMAN

Even He that died for us upon the cross,

in the last hour...was mindful of His Mother, as if to

teach us that this holy love should be our last

worldly thought, the last point of earth from which

the soul should take its flight for heaven.

HENRY WADSWORTH LONGFELLOW

Our mother's life drew together so many Christlike characteristics that the Bible praises and the world desperately needs. Always manifesting unruffled strength and gentleness, her love for God and her faith in God were unshakeable. Mum trusted God for each one of her children. She prayed for us, believed in us, and loved all of us unconditionally. We are fulfilling our God-given destinies because our mother dedicated her life to bringing us up in the way of the Lord. As a grandma she somehow planted herself forever in each grandchild's young heart. She has finished her time here on earth, but her influence keeps flowing on down through her children and her grandchildren. One can only imagine the beauty of our mum as she worships around the eternal throne.

We love you, Mum.

JEAN, LYNNE, AND RUTH

A mother can read all the child-rearing books and can subscribe to any theory of parenting, but what gets passed along to her children is something far more intimate and mysterious than anything contained therein. What gets passed along is her character, and it enters into her kids as surely and as inexorably as water flows from a fuller vessel into a less-full one.

LAURENCE SHAMES

I am not in any doubt as to how my own Christian experience began. The altar before which I knelt first was my mother's knee.

L. D. WEATHERHEAD

A mother's love is unlike any other kind of love. Its expression and depth cannot be matched for it is a gift from God.

AUTHOR UNKNOWN

Say to mothers, what a holy charge

is theirs; with what a kingly power

their love might rule the fountains

of the newborn mind.

LYDIA HUNTLEY SIGOURNEY

Judicious mothers

will always keep in mind that they

are the first book read, and the last

put aside in every child's library.

C. LENOX REDMOND

Mother did not think of herself as deeply spiritual. She would have protested if anyone had said she was. But she was certainly hungry for God, deeply conscious of her own...need of Him. Called to be a mother, entrusted with the holy task of cooperating with God in shaping the destinies of six people, she knew it was too heavy a burden to carry alone. She did not try. She went to Him whose name is Wonderful Counsellor, Mighty God, Everlasting Father. She asked His help—daily.

ELISABETH ELLIOT
THE SHAPING OF A CHRISTIAN FAMILY

Mother taught me to see God's fingerprints on the world around me. But even more importantly, she taught me to look for God in the pages of his Word. And it seemed to me, even as a child, that every time my mother opened her Bible, she found something new about God. And she would tell her children what she had found.

Those childhood images my mother created for me are forever fixed in my mind—in my thoughts about the person Jesus is and the God He came to earth to represent. My mother taught theology in pictures. And she was always saying, "Can't you just see God?..."

But when all the sights and sounds of longing are cleared away, I return to the simple gift my mother gave me—the ability to see God's gifts all around me and then quietly sit back, enjoy, and give thanks for what He's given.

It is perhaps my mother's greatest legacy to me.

And I am a more contented person because of it.

RUTH SENTER

A Mother's Heart

Oh, if there be in retrospection's chain

One link that knits us

with young dreams again,

One thought so sweet,

we scarcely dare muse

On all the hoarded rapture it reviews—

Which seems each instant

in its backward range,

The heart to soften and its ties to chain,

And every spring, untouched

for years, to move—

It is the memory of a mother's love.

ANONYMOUS

If there be aught

Surpassing human deed or word, or thought,

It is a mother's love.

MARCHIONESS DE SPADARA

Where There Is Love

My mother was an angel upon earth.

She was a minister of blessing to all

human beings within her sphere of action.

She had no feelings but of kindness and

beneficence, yet her mind was as firm

as her temper was mild and gentle.

JOHN QUINCY ADAMS

Her love is like an island

In life's ocean, vast and wide,

A peaceful, quiet shelter

From the wind, and rain, and tide.

'Tis bound on the north by Hope,

By Patience on the west,

By tender Counsel on the south,

And on the east by Rest.

Above is like a beacon light,

Shining Faith, and Truth, and Prayer;

And through the changing scenes of life,

I find a haven there.

AUTHOR UNKNOWN

I have been handed a great legacy by my mother. She has given me life, love, security, confidence, encouragement, companionship, advice, reverence for God. It wasn't until I visited, for the first time as an adult, my grandmother's grave, that I felt the true impact of my mother's life. The words carved on my grandmother's tombstone were, "She died as she lived, trusting in Jesus." My grandmother's trust was honored, for her children and her grandchildren are all committed Christians. What greater legacy could a child ask for?

RUTH LENTER AND JOY LENTER STUART

Who are

the best spokespersons

about being a mother?

Perhaps it's mothers themselves

who can best put into simple words

the way in which a mother influences lives.

Reflect upon how your mother influenced

you and how you too are shaping

the next generation.

AUTHOR UNKNOWN

$\mathcal{T}$his is how we get back up when we have fallen...

This is who God is and how he works in our lives...

"Things that we have heard and know, that our fathers (and

mothers) have told us. We will not hide them from our

children, but tell to the coming generation the glorious

deeds of the Lord, and his might...which he commanded to

our fathers (and mothers) to teach to their children; that the

next generation might know them, the children yet unborn,

and arise and tell them to their children, so that they

should set their hope in God..." (Psalm 78:3-6).

This is my work, my calling, for the decades ahead. And

this I learned from my mother. She taught (and teaches me

still) how to be a good grandmother.

KAREN BURTON MAINS

$\mathcal{M}$om's devotion to God and her wholehearted determination to spend her life serving Him has challenged me in my Christian walk. I've always marveled at how reading the Bible and praying is so integrated with trying to find the "right" time to have a quiet time. What Mom has taught me is that there probably isn't just one right time. I need to grab the moment each day.

JUDY BRISCOE GOLZ

My mother was a model of moral and ethical standards—both in principle and in practice—and she shared those convictions with me. She laid down guidelines and boundaries for me, but again it was not what she did in a structured way as much as who she was that really made the difference.

Her attitude toward me was always one of trust.

My mother's willingness to trust me has given me an incredible gift. God used my mother and that trust to give me a sense of security. God also used my mother to teach me to have fun—not as a separate event but as an integral part of all the work, the responsibility, and even the agonies of parenting.

COLLEEN TOWNSEND EVANS

$\mathcal{M}$y mama uses her stories to grow roots

of joy and connectedness.

My mama's stories make every listener feel deeply

cherished, never humiliated or criticized. Her stories

are an act of worship, a declaration that each person

matters and that each event in life is important.

KAREN DOCKREY

There is nothing

more beautiful in the world

than a mother who places

her heart in the Lord.

BONNIE JENSEN

All that I am or hope to be

I owe to my angel mother.

ABRAHAM LINCOLN

But, the most remarkable thing about my Mom has been, and still is, her faith—her unwavering faith-born ability to see beyond any circumstance and make the best of it, even the most difficult situations. She loves God and knows Him intimately. She knows the power of prayer and keeps believing in God's touch and intervention for her family, even though we're all in our forties and fifties now. And all through my growing-up years she instilled that same faith in me.

How has she influenced my life? I can't think of one single way she hasn't. Many times I've said thank you. I'm grateful for the opportunity to say it again.

Thanks, Mom. Thanks for being simple, loving, remarkable, irreplaceable you.

NEVA COYLE

It seems but yesterday
you lay
new in my arms.
Into our lives you brought
sunshine and laughter—
play—
showers, too,
and song.
Headstrong,
heart strong,
gay,
tender beyond believing,
simple in faith,
clear-eyed,
shy,
eager for life—
you left us
rich in memories,
little wife.
And now today
I hear you say
words beyond your years.
I watch you play
with your small son,
tenderest of mothers.
Years slip away—
today
we are mothers
together.

RUTH BELL GRAHAM

*Years slip away—
today
we are mothers
together.*

Mother lives in her grandchildren's memories (as I am determined I will weave my life into the memories of my grandchildren). There are many gifts my mother gave to me, but the one which I'm only beginning to realize is this: my mother taught me how to be a good grandmother.

Obviously, this is an art, lore best passed from generation to generation. And it seems to me that good grandmothering consists of many things. It is intentionally creating happy memories for all the decades that follow; it is a matter of providing joyful learning experiences; it is a spiritual calling to pass on the values that conserve the Christian ethos. But most of all, as millions of grandparents testify, it is a way of delight.

My mother knew that she was the connective tissue of history. Knowledge of what has been and of how to do would be lost if she hadn't bestowed it. And I hear myself passing on her wisdom as she passed it on to me.

KAREN BURTON MAINS

Three Cheers for Mother!

Over the centuries she's worked as hard
as father and for very different reasons.

He has built the houses; she's added the colors,
the smells, the music.

He has shaped constitutions to make citizens protected;
she has sewn flags to make them weep and cheer.

He has mustered armies and police forces to put down
oppression; she has prayed for them and patted them on
the back and sent them off with their heads up.

He has shaped decisions; she has added morale.

Celebrate the mother! She, too, no less than the father,
has, under God, shaped a magnificent human tradition.

ANNE ORTLUND